MW00810907

How to Make a Six-Figure Income Working Part-Time

How to Make a Six-Figure Income Working Part-Time

Rebecca Whitman

Copyright ©2018 by Rebecca Whitman

All rights reserved. This book or any portion thereof may not be reproduced or used in any manner whatsoever without the express written permission of the publisher except for the use of brief quotations in a book review.

Printed in the United States of America

First Printing, 2018

ISBN-13: 978-1-947637-98-6 print edition
ISBN-13: 978-1-947637-99-3 ebook edition

Waterside Press
2055 Oxford Ave
Cardiff, CA 92007
www.waterside.com

*"In Loving Memory of
My Father - Roy Whitman, MD"*

CONTENTS

FOREWORD

As I sit here on a Friday night, I am 46 years old, I am newly divorced and my father just passed away, I should be devastated. But, instead, due to the principles in this book, I am actually the happiest I have ever been in my life. I have reached a new level of surrender, of knowing that I am not in control. That is not a burden, but a relief. I did my best job to meet the right people, go to the right parties, and attend the right schools to get a specific result. A result that I am not even sure I wanted. My parents, my friends, and my society told me that I need to marry a wealthy man and have kids in order to be happy. I have failed miserably at both. So why am I happy? That is what we will explore in this book.

I believe that happy is the new rich. How many people do you know that did all the right things? They have the money, the family and the social status, but they are miserable. Life is short. In the scope of the Universe and eternity, we are here for a nanosecond. Don't you want to take what is left of the rest of your life and be happy? How many years have you wasted making other people happy to your own detriment? It is now time to pause and ask yourself some simple questions.

What do I want?
How do I feel in my current circumstances?
What action is needed, if any, to get me to what I want?

We all know when something is no longer working for us. Whether it is a job, a relationship, a car, a home, or even a city where we reside. If we stay open to the signs that are all around us, they will point to the fact that change is needed.

One of my favorite spiritual teachers, Michael Bernard Beckwith, founder of the Agape International Spiritual Center, says that there are only two ways that people change. "They are either pushed by pain, or pulled by a vision." If my goal in life is to be happy, so that I can then be of service to my fellows, I have to be willing to walk away from the people, places and situations that no longer serve my highest good. Michael also explains that transformation is more of a process of subtraction. But in society we are taught that happiness comes through addition. If I can just acquire more stuff, then I will be happy. It is up to you how much emotional pain you will have to endure before you make a change.

The only constant in this life is change. How well we adapt to change determines the level of our happiness. When I accept change or even celebrate it, rather than resist it, I can find happiness in any situation. People who resist change often suffer from premature aging and poor health. Disease is really dis-ease. If your mind is not at ease, your body and your spirit will not be at ease either. How would you like to experience a clear mind and vibrant health? That is what we will be striving for in this book.

As much as I miss my dad, death does not have to be perceived as a loss. In fact, one of my favorite spiritual teachings from Abraham Hicks calls death "a joyous reemergence with divine Love". My dad was 91 when he made his transition. He lived a wonderfully full and successful life. I can celebrate his life and who he was in the world. I can be grateful that I am still on the planet. One of the reasons I chose to write this book was his constant encouragement for me to write something. He was an accomplished academic in the field of psychiatry and wrote hundreds of published articles. To honor his memory, I would like to give writing a shot. I hope you enjoy my effort!

Rebecca Whitman
2018

INTRODUCTION

"We spend our youth attaining wealth and our wealth attaining youth." - Douglas Copeland

This book is about attaining that ever elusive work-life balance. Everyone's work-life balance is going to look different because we all have different priorities. Let's contemplate the quote above from Douglas Copeland, who has written amazing books about generational psychology. "We spend our youth attaining wealth." We were taught to go to school, get good grades, go to college and then we would be rich. I distinctly remember a poster while I was in college and it had a six-car garage full of luxury cars and read, "Justification for a Higher Education".

When I graduated from Princeton University, I thought I was going to get any job I wanted. What happened was I moved to New York City and all that was offered to me was internships. "Internships?", I thought to myself. How ridiculous! I was brainwashed into thinking by going to the Ivy League, I was a leader. Shouldn't they be offering me a paid job? I mean, how else was I going to support myself in Manhattan?

I was just too proud to accept an unpaid internship, so I started walking around my neighborhood, on the Upper West Side, and filling out applications at local restaurants.

I couldn't believe how rude both the customers and my boss were to me. After getting fired from two restaurants, for being "too nice" and "too sensitive", I started looking for jobs in the "Help Wanted" section of the newspaper. This was in 1993, before the internet job sites. After circling an ad that said, "Circle Me", I set up an interview. Little did I know it was a group overview to convince me to join a network marketing company. If you don't know what that is, it's one of those "pyramid deals", you know, like *Amway* or *Mary Kay*.

The company was called *Equinox International*. They had a line of nutritional products, as well as water and air filtration. Everything the owner of that company, Bill Gouldd, predicted came true. He said that cancer, diabetes and heart disease would become epidemics. That has surely happened. He said that we were destroying our water supply and polluting our environment to the point of no repair. The best solution was to protect yourself with water and air filters. I thought what he said made sense and I wasn't getting any other offers, so I joined his company. Many of the general sales concepts that are explained in this book I learned from attending his training company's 'Advanced Marketing Seminars'. He has gotten a lot of bad press, because many people lost money buying the products and not being able to resell them. But I can only thank this man for being a powerful mentor in the formative years of my early twenties.

Princeton had taught me to be a free thinker and to question everything. Bill Gouldd questioned everything, too. He would ask, "What kind of life do you want? Do you want to follow the mindless masses?" Their program says work at least 40 hours, for 40 years and if you are lucky you will end up with a gold watch and a pension plan. Maybe, if you are a model employee, they will honor your years of sacrifice with a pitiful retirement party, before they send you out to pasture to die.

The point of work is not just to make money. If you spend all your life making money and then die, you have no time to enjoy the fruits of your labor. Do you want to live to work, as in the paradigm I mentioned above, or do you want to work to live? I want to work to live a full, joyous life.

I am not motivated by money. What is money exactly? It is paper and metal, literally. What money is to me is freedom. I don't want to be in prison for 40 years, working 40 hours a week. I don't want to be told when to take a lunch break or when I can take my two weeks of vacation. I don't want to be written up and given a pink slip, if I am five minutes late for work. We are all programmed to work for corporations by our school system. We are taught to wake up early, take the bus, sit in school, not because we want to be there, but because we have to be.

We are taught to follow the rules, not call attention to ourselves, to wait in line and, if we follow all the rules and regurgitate what the teacher tells us is important, we get an "A". Our happiness is not at all considered in the process.

In my opinion, your level of happiness and freedom is the true "A" on the only report card that matters, your life. My definition of freedom is the ability to do what I want, when I want, where I want and with who I want. If I am doing anything out of obligation or fear, I am not being my best self. When I show up and I want to be present, you get the best version of me. When I show up out of guilt or obligation, I will be there in body, but my spirit will be dimmed. People can sense when you don't want to be there, no matter how good an actor you think you are.

I am from 'Generation X', which is people born between the years 1961 to 1981. Generation X was the first generation to feel like we had a choice whether to climb the corporate ladder or not. You might say the same thing about the hippies from the 'Baby Boomer' generation. They had strong ideals about freedom, but most of them sold out when they realized the expense of having a family. Of course, there still some tried and true hippies. Most of them live in Venice, where I currently reside. I think Generation X rebelled from their hard working parents. We are the generation that doesn't want to grow up. We are the generation that knew we would never make as much money as our parents or have the lifestyle our parents had. The whole "slacker" phenomenon came from Gen Xers that didn't see the point of allowing work to form the man. Slackers are the modern day nihilistic existentialists.

We were the first generation that asked ourselves, "Do we really want to throw our life away working for somebody else?" We watched our parents work so hard to provide for their families, but they were miserable. We wanted work to be just one of the spokes in our wheel of life not the whole wheel as it has been in previous generations. The whole *Starbucks* and 'coffee house culture' came from the idea that it is, actually, okay just to sit in a café for hours on end and drink coffee. We don't always have to be gunning for some huge goal. Although, with technology, people now use coffee shops as their offices.

I believe that people are more interested in creating memories than materialism. Not every woman feels compelled to have kids. Not every couple be they gay or straight feels the need to have kids. So people are traveling more than ever. More people are seeking spirituality and personal growth than ever before. More people are exercising and doing yoga than ever before. People are being less judgmental of different lifestyles than ever before. People are accepting of different sexual orientations more than ever.

More and more people are meditating. The love revolution is happening. You can see it in movies, television and commercials. The whole world is waking up. There is a rise in people's consciousness about what it means to be a human and the importance of making a difference in the world.

My goal in this book is to teach you to make the most amount of money you can, while working the least amount of hours. For the past decade I have been able to make a six figure income, while working part time. I have been able to travel, and to take as much time off as I wanted. I was able to spend quality time with my father in the last few years of his life. I have gotten into the best shape of my life, as I have plenty of time to exercise. I have never looked younger or happier. Happy is the best face lift in town. You can't bottle radiance. I have had the money to get massages, acupuncture and take the best nutritional supplements to maximize my health. I have had time to walk my dog, for over an hour a day, and enjoy nature and animal kinship. I have been able to sleep eight hours a night. You don't have to be stressed or live an unhealthy lifestyle to make money. I am not a gazillionare, but that is not my goal. I am interested in being as happy and as healthy as I can be, while making money. Money is not as important as lifestyle.

Through the principles in this book, you will learn how to be your best self in several poignant areas:

1. Spiritual
2. Physical
3. Emotional
4. Mental

5. Social
6. Romantic
7. Financial

We will explore each area in the following chapters. They are in that order for a reason. You will get three affirmations to say aloud to yourself several times a day, as you are working on each area. Affirmations are a great way to reprogram your negative self-talk. Don't just say these affirmations by rote. Say them with positive emotion as if they are already happening in your life. If you are in commission based sales or in your own business, I am going to teach you how to make a six-figure income working part time. If you are in any field of work, you will learn how to maximize your income while you maximize your joy!

1 Spirituality

"My religion is simple. My religion is kindness."
- Dalai Lama

The cornerstone for creating a beautifully balanced life is spirituality. Without peace of mind, you can have all the money in the world and remain miserable. You can have the perfect relationship and not enjoy it; or even worse, sabotage it with your negative attitude. Some of the most talented, wealthy and beloved entertainers in the world kill themselves, because they built a life without putting in the foundation first their spiritual life.

When you are building a house, the longest and most arduous phase is creating the foundation. Once you have that piece in place the rest of the building goes up very quickly in comparison. In this fast paced, high-tech society, a lot of people feel they don't have the time to nurture a spiritual life. It is so ironic that all this technology was invented with the idea of making our lives more efficient and convenient. But instead of using the extra time to connect with each other and with our spirit, we are just filling up our days with distractions. We are so addicted to checking our social media, email and the news, that it is challenging to create the space to renew our souls. I encourage you to turn off your phone and schedule the time to relax and rejuvenate your soul.

First, you must create a Higher Power of your own understanding, as is accepted in those 'Twelve Steps'. My Higher Power isn't a male figure on the throne keeping track of who has been naughty or nice, like Santa Claus. My Higher Power does not judge or punish me. That is the type of God that many of us were familiar with growing up in a Judeo-Christian culture. Instead, my God is Love. We can't see, taste, or touch God with our five senses, but we all know exactly what love is. Love is a feeling, a state of mind, a way of being in the world. We can relate to the love we feel for a pet or a child. We can feel love for a friend or neighbor. We can love an ideal or a community. We can love our country and the ideals it was founded upon. We know what romantic love feels like. We know the love we have for our parents, elders, teachers and coaches. It all falls under one big category, LOVE. Love is the higher road. When confused about a circumstance or situation, ask yourself, "What would Love do? How would Love react to that person? How would Love handle that situation?" The answers will be easy to decipher.

I agree with the Schucman's Course in Miracles that there are two primary emotions from which all other emotions spring - love and fear. We live in a fear-based society. We are being bombarded with messages from advertisers that we are not good enough. We are not good-looking enough, young enough, cool enough, popular enough, fun enough, unless we buy their product. Buying something to fix what's wrong with us is the basis of consumerism. What if you decided today that you are already enough? That no product, home, lover or vacation will fix you. There is absolutely nothing missing from your life. People in developing countries are significantly happier than people in First World countries, because they are not programmed to be in a constant state of acquisition. They are not seeking anything outside of themselves to fix them. They delight in the simple joys of life.

In the First World, all of our basic needs are met, like food, shelter, and water so we preoccupy our minds with getting more, more, more. More of everything is valued in our society. More attention, more money, more accolades, more friends, more travel, more stuff. And no matter how much we get, it's never enough. You can break free of this fear-driven consumerism by deciding that you don't need anything. All you want can be found within you!

When you make the conscious decision to switch your bottom line emotion from fear to love, don't expect your friends and family to applaud you. Many of your friends and family like when you are depressed. It makes them feel better about themselves. It's like the old saying "misery loves company". If you get too happy, then they have to look at themselves. When they see your smiling, happy face you are reflecting back to them their own unhappiness. The last person in the world you want to see when you are down is a happy person. So when you take on this new attitude, don't be surprised if some of your friends go away. My favorite quote by master teacher Wayne Dyer is, "Love is my gift to the world. I fill myself with Love. And I send that Love out into the world. How others treat me is their path. How I react is mine."

Affirmations can be very useful to reprogram your negative thought patterns. I recommend writing down a list of your fears. And for each fear you can write an affirmation that counteracts it. For example, if you struggle with the core belief of not feeling good enough, you can use the affirmation "I am enough". Here is a list of affirmations that I personally use to counter my negative beliefs about myself.

I am not what I have. I am not what I do.

I am not my age, my height, my weight, or my dress size.

I am not my relationship with men.

I am not what other people think of me.

I am not my society.

I am what I am and it's enough.

I am as God created me.

All my needs are always met.

All things are working together for my highest good.

Everything I do comes easily, effortlessly, and elegantly.

Everything in the Universe is for me.

And nothing is against me. Life is supposed to be fun.

I stop taking myself so damn seriously.

I stop fighting anyone or anything - even you.

Thanks, God!

Meditation is also a crucial component to living a God-centered life. Our minds are so accustomed to racing, it is difficult at first to slow them down. There is no right or wrong way to meditate. Just find some time to settle down in your body. They always say your back should be upright, but I prefer laying down or just having my shoulders on a pillow. I really enjoy listening to the app "Insight Timer". It has a huge catalogue of guided meditations. If you don't know how to meditate, they make it so simple. All you have to do is listen. They have mediations for every area of your life, eating healthy, sleeping, relationships, health, and more. They also have podcasts and tutorials for how to meditate. I also like saying an affirmation or mantra to myself as I meditate. On the inhale I say to myself "All is well", and on the exhale

I say "I have everything I need". Just being quiet and focusing on your breath is meditation. I like to use the timer on my cell phone, in case I am running short on time and so I don't fall asleep. Praying is talking to God. Mediating is listening to God. You can ask your Higher Power a question and just listen during your meditation. You will be surprised and delighted how quickly the answers will come to you. I believe we all have a deep, innate knowing. Meditation puts you in touch with your powerful, inner wisdom.

Creating a morning ritual is an important aspect to living the spiritual life. Before you even get out of bed, you can thank God for waking you up. Do you have any idea how many millions of people die each night and don't have the privilege of waking up? Do you have a clue how many other millions of people were closely connected to those who died last night? If you haven't lost a loved one you have much to be grateful for. You can take a moment to bask in the joy of just being alive on the planet before you get out of bed.

Meister Eckhart said that, "If the only prayer you ever said in your entire life was thank you, that would suffice". Some people hit their knees and ask that God be in charge of their day. A good trick to make yourself do this is to hide your keys under your bed. If you aren't comfortable praying on your knees, you can just connect to your Higher Power in your own way. You can also lie in bed and set an intention for your day. By the time you hit the toilet, some kind of contact can be made.

To keep this conscious contact going with your Higher Power, I recommend turning your car into your own temple. This is a positive way to make the most of your commute to work and get the right mindset for the day. There are so many CDs, podcasts, and uplifting music that can make your time in traffic a benefit to your spiritual life. We have had so many years of programming that teaches us to be negative and fearful. It takes constant vigilance to change those old negative messages into positive ones. When your mind is focused on the past, you feel depressed. When you focus on the future, you feel anxious. Your happiness lies in the present moment.

So few people enjoy their lives in the moment. Before they know it, they are on their death beds, wondering where did the time go? To ground yourself in the moment, focus on your five senses. What are your eyes seeing in this moment? Look at the colors of trees, flowers, your loved ones and all the nuances of design and movement. What are you hearing? Music is a wonderful tool to shift your mood and keep you happy in the moment. What are you smelling? Food, flowers, incense, and candles are all wonderful ways to bask in the moment. What are you feeling? Are you petting your animal companion, feeling a piece of fruit to determine if its ripe, or embracing a loved one? What are you tasting? Some people eat so fast that they don't even taste their food. Really savor each bite and taste all the preparation that went into the food. Many people have an altar in their home where they have articles that help them feel connected to Spirit, like crystals, candles, statues, pictures or incense.

How you start and end your day is really important. Some people have music they play or a theme song to help them start their day off on the right foot. You can listen to your favorite spiritual teachers on *YouTube* or *Hay House Radio*, or on a podcast as you are getting ready for work.

Many people wake up and go to bed with the news on. That is programming your mind for doom and gloom. What you watch right before you go to bed goes directly into your subconscious mind. Your mental defenses go down when you are asleep, and your mind absorbs all the negativity from the news. I do believe that we should be up to date with what is happening in the world. I prefer to get my news on the internet or if you prefer the newspaper is fine, too. Just not in the moments before you fall asleep.

Some people like to read from daily mediation books or spiritual literature before they fall asleep, or when they wake up. However you decide to honor your spiritual side is up to you. The morning ritual is the most important. How you start your day usually determines what kind of day you will have. If you can just set aside five minutes in the morning to connect with your Higher Power, you will set yourself up for a great day. I also believe you can start your day over anytime, if you feel yourself getting off track. You can read something inspirational on the internet, or take a few minutes in your car to just close your eyes and reconnect with your breath.

Another important aspect of spirituality is community. It is very boring to be spiritual all by yourself in your home. Fellowship and socializing with likeminded people makes the spiritual life dynamic and fun. Whether it's your temple, church, 12 Steps meetings, seminars, or yoga class, your community is out there. Your vibe attracts your tribe. Doing classes, workshops, and retreats help you bond with likeminded individuals.

I believe that God speaks through other people. If I attend a class or go out to eat with people, I am listening with bated breath to the pearl of wisdom that will come out of someone's mouth when I least expect it. If I am checking my phone, I might just miss the next piece of information to get me to the next level of my spiritual journey. Listening is the best gift I could give others and myself. It's amazing what you can learn and how attractive you are if you can just be an active listener. You can ask people how they are and how you can be of service to them. It is a great way to get out of your own way. We are so self-obsessed these days. We live in such a narcissistic, look-at-me culture. I am so sick of myself. I have endlessly analyzed how I think, how I look, what I want. When I am with my community it is so much more interesting to learn about how others are living their truth, and moving through the world.

AFFIRMATIONS

I AM A SPIRITUAL BEING HAVING A
HUMAN EXPERIENCE.

I HAVE A CONNECTION TO THE
DIVINE THAT GIVES ME PEACE
AND EASE.

I AM ABLE TO GO WITH THE FLOW
AND KNOW THAT EVERYTHING
WORKS OUT FOR ME.

2 FITNESS

"It is health that is the real wealth and not pieces of gold and silver." - Mahatma Gandhi

They say "health is the new wealth and happy is the new rich". I believe the two go hand in hand. I also like the saying, "move a muscle, change a thought". I challenge you to be sad after an invigorating cardio session with music you adore. I believe that the endorphins, dopamine, and serotonin you get from a great workout are more powerful than psycho-active drugs.

Don't get me wrong. If you are taking anti-depressants, please consult with a medical professional before getting off your medication. But I do believe medication is over-prescribed.

One in six Americans is taking some kind of psychiatric drug. Most of them are for depression, anxiety or sleep. Exercise can help with all of those. There are so many ways to work out today. People used to think that exercise is boring. You can switch up your workouts to keep them exciting. There are live streamed workouts, podcasts, videos, gyms, and more private fitness studios than ever before. It is socially acceptable to wear workout clothes anywhere.

Yoga pants are even being worn into the workplace. Exercise used to be only for famous actors who wanted to look good for the camera. Now everyone has access to the same type of workouts the stars do. You used to have to hire a personal trainer to transform your body and get results. Not anymore. You can take body sculpting classes and read books on nutrition to get the same results as your favorite celebrities.

Nutrition also plays a huge part in feeling good. Your body is like a high performance car. If you put water in the tank of a Ferrari, it would not drive the way it would if you put premium gasoline in it. So many people are going so fast that they don't take the time to eat healthy. I am not a good cook. But I can still watch what I eat. I am vegan for health and moral reasons. But you don't have to be a vegan to eat healthy. You can buy free range eggs or grass-fed meats. Whole Foods and Trader Joe's have so many healthy meals that are pre-prepared, all you have to do is heat them up. We can all drink more water and eat more fruits and vegetables. If you don't have the time to cook your vegetables, you can drink them in a smoothie, juice, take them in powder or capsule form. There are now meal prep services that will make a week's worth of food for you and deliver it right to your door. There are more health-conscious options in almost all restaurants. You don't have to become obsessive with diet to the point where you can't enjoy going out to eat or to a dinner party. Just make healthier choices. Don't just eat to numb emotions or out of boredom. Being aware of what you put into your body is key.

Keeping a food diary is a great way to create some awareness around food. There are many apps that track calories, how much water you drink and how much exercise you do. If you can't stop obsessing about food, there are support groups that can help you. Weight Watchers, Jenny Craig, and Overeaters Anonymous can offer both community and individual support. You don't have to do this alone. When people buy a product, concept or service from you, they are buying you. If you don't feel good in your body, you will not emanate the confidence you need to gain their trust. Heart disease, cancer, and diabetes are at an all-time high. Scientific studies have linked these deadly epidemics to what we eat. The drugs that treat these diseases are a billion-dollar industry. It's time to stop spending your hard-earned money on drugs to treat your health and invest that money in healthy food and exercise so you don't need to be on drugs. As the famous philosopher Hippocrates said, "Let the food be thy medicine and medicine be thy food."

Now, I am not saying if you are taking a medication for a health issue to stop taking it immediately. That would be scary. Just ask your doctor if there are any medications from which you might be able to slowly wean yourself off. And in the meantime, go to a holistic doctor, a homeopathic clinic or do acupuncture. Chinese medicine has been around for over 5,000 years and Western medicine has been around for a couple of hundred years. China does not have the epidemic of obesity, they don't have the Chinese Diabetes or Heart Associations. Why not glean from their wellspring of medical knowledge? A good acupuncturist can get you on a regimen of treatments and herbs that could help you get off some synthetic drugs. Chinese herbs won't destroy your liver, like synthetic drugs.

Massage is also a great way to keep your body feeling its best. There are so many inexpensive ways to get a massage. Most insurance plans now have coverage for acupuncture and massage. There are chains like Burke Williams and Massage Envy, where you can get a membership to reduce the cost of a regular massage. There are Chinese foot massage shops where they soak your feet, but they also massage your whole body for about $20 an hour. You can get a great Thai massage, where they walk on your back for around $40 an hour. Many chiropractors and physical therapy clinics offer sports massage at a reasonable rate. If you are working hard to build your business, and working out regularly, I recommend getting a massage a minimum of twice a month. Once a week would be ideal. I know it seems like an unnecessary expense if you are not accustomed to getting a regular massage. But the hours of productivity you gain from feeling great in your body, will more than make up for it. Wouldn't you rather invest some extra money in your health now when you can enjoy it? Or would you want to eat, drink and smoke to your heart's content now, and spend all your time and money fighting off a serious medical problem later? Obviously, you would want to go out of your way to maximize your health now.

I am not talking about depriving yourself. I believe everything can be enjoyed in moderation. If you tell yourself that no matter what you do, you will not eat the chocolate cake in the refrigerator, then all you will do is obsess on eating the chocolate cake. Allow yourself to have a couple of bites of the cake. The women in European countries like France and Italy are gorgeous and slim for the most part. They eat bread, cheese and dessert. They know how to enjoy food because they allow themselves to eat whatever they want. Then afterwards they don't beat themselves up about it, like American women do. It's called portion control. In addition to moderation, I don't believe in using a scale. I have personally never got off a scale and felt good about myself. My goal weight is sexy as fuck. I like the saying "strong is the new skinny".

Society has oppressed women by making their value by their age, appearance, especially their weight. Only a small percentage of the women have the naturally skinny body type, that is so celebrated in the fashion magazines. The rest of the models that look that emaciated are anorexic. We can thank Kim Kardashian, Jennifer Lopez and Beyoncé for making curves trendy. They actually look like real women and have shapes that we can all be inspired by. Being in shape is not about conforming to some unrealistic beauty ideal, but to feel the best you can in your body. There are many clothing lines for plus size women and the models representing them look like goddesses. You can rock your curves or rock your lack of curves. As long as you feel good about yourself, that is what matters. Your confidence is what gets you attention, not your dress size.

I did a lingerie shoot a couple years ago to celebrate freeing myself from a toxic marriage. The photographer told me that the women who enjoy the shoot the most and feel the most comfortable in their bodies are Latina and African American women. While the women with an almost perfect shape, by society's standard, were not having as much fun and focused on their every flaw. Why is that? I believe that women from minority cultures are more cherished and complimented for their natural beauty than Caucasian women. White women feel like unless they look like they stepped off the runway, they don't look good enough.

These body ideals were contrived by gay men on Madison Avenue that wanted women to look like adolescent boys. Society has created an impossible ideal, that most women strive for their whole lives and never achieve. This is a way to control women; by making them feel badly about themselves and disempowered. Men judge women and women judge other women's worth by their weight. For women to be their best selves, this judgment has got to stop! Real women have curves. I don't want to exercise to be skinny. I want to be a lean, bad ass. When I got my photos back from this lingerie shoot, I could barely recognize myself. Not only was my body in the best shape of my life, I was glowing with happiness.

Body shaming is a big trend on the internet. Most of the people on the internet that are critiquing celebrities for not having a perfect body, aren't even in shape. Let's stop body shaming people and start celebrating them for being a unique expression of divine beauty. If we all looked exactly the same, and dressed exactly the same, life would be so boring. It is okay to be motivated to exercise to get your body to the next level, but don't forget to be thankful that you have a healthy body that got you this far on your life's journey. Many people are disabled and unable to exercise at all. What a privilege it is to be able to move your body, to sweat, and to feel your heart beating. I like dedicating my work out to someone I know that doesn't have the capacity to work out. My dad was always a great athlete. The last couple years of his life his legs gave out and he couldn't walk or stand without people helping him. I would think of him in spin class and pedal for him. He would have done anything to have use of his legs again. Who can you dedicate your workout to?

Some people are gym rats, but others prefer to exercise outside. Most cell phones come equipped these days with pedometers. You can set a daily goal of how many steps a day you want to walk. Ten thousand steps is five miles. Even 2500 steps would change your fitness dramatically, if you are accustomed to being sedentary. If you are too busy to hit the gym, we can all find the time to do some more walking. You can park farther away from your destination. You can skip the valet service. You can bike or walk to work. You can take the steps instead of the elevator.

15

Walking or hiking in nature is great exercise and it is good for the soul. Taking your dog with you on a hike makes it even more fun. Or you can invite a friend or group of friends on the hike and enjoy talking while you walk. Before you know it, you have walked miles, but you were so lost in conversation that you didn't even realize it. People join walking, hiking and running clubs for this reason. There are also 'Meet Up' groups for virtually every sport. Misery loves company. If you are exercising in a group, you can feed off the other people's energy and get inspired by them. There's nothing like fresh air and observing the beauty of nature to keep you grounded in the present moment. If you work out with a friend, trainer or sign up for a class you have accountability. It is too easy to say you don't have time to exercise, unless you have made a commitment to exercise with someone.

When you do make the time to exercise, reward yourself with a healthy smoothie, coffee or even a new workout outfit. There were many times I didn't want to work out. But I told myself if I just exercise for half an hour, I will buy myself a boba tea or a smoothie. It works! No one ever left the gym saying "I wish I would not have made the time to exercise today!" Just getting to the gym is more than half the battle. Once you create the habit of exercising, it becomes a part of your lifestyle, like eating or taking a shower. You would never think to miss a meal or a shower. It is just part of what you do on a daily basis to take care of yourself. The most important thing is to find an exercise you like to do because it is fun. My father, who played tennis well into his eighties said, "sweat once a day". You can do it!

AFFIRMATIONS

I AM EXPERIENCING RADIANT
HEALTH.

I HAVE MORE THAN ENOUGH ENERGY
TO EXERCISE DAILY.

I AM ABLE TO GET STRONGER AND
BETTER EVERY TIME I MOVE
MY BODY.

3 EMOTIONAL

"A friend is someone who gives you total freedom to be yourself." - Jim Morrison

In order to be successful in anything, you have to know why you want it. Finding your why is an important step in the climb to success. Are you motivated to pay for your children's college tuition? Do you want to retire early? Are you providing care for an elderly parent? Are you on a mission to change the world? Success has an emotional component. If it is just material accumulation, you can get burned out and easily discouraged. We all have enough stuff. As long as we have our basic needs covered, like food, shelter, clothes, cell phone and a car, we can feel comfortable. It is so easy to just be satisfied paying our bills and living pay check to pay check. But if you want to achieve wealth, you need a driving force. That drive comes from your why. You can put this book down and set the timer on your phone for just ten minutes and ask yourself, "Why do I want to be successful?" Write down whatever comes to mind without judging it. Let your subconscious do the talking for once. It knows what you really want. Trust it.

Once you determine why you want wealth, you now need to surround yourself with like-minded people who support your mission. There's an old saying that "You are who you hang around". People usually hang out with people who make within ten percent of their income bracket. So, an easy way to make a shift is to befriend a successful person. If you ask them, you might be lucky enough to have them as a mentor. An easy formula for success in every area of your life is to find someone who has what you want and if you do what they did, you can get what they got. Another term for this is match and model. This is how babies learn to walk, talk and even think. If there is someone who is successful in your chosen field, ask them if you can just shadow them for a few weeks to learn their techniques.

I remember when I was doing live sales presentations for a company. I was the top money earner in that organization. One of my co-workers was desperate to make more money. He was also a professional cameraman. He asked if he could record me doing a sales presentation. Of course I said yes. He got my presentation on tape, memorized it, and started to quadruple his income. He simply repeated my sales pitch verbatim.

Your friends have a huge influence on your success. Many people are in the habit of complaining and commiserating with their friends. If you stop griping to these people, you might not have anything to talk about. Your words are your advertisement to the boundaries of the Universe. If you want the same lousy results, keep complaining. The author Carl Greer wrote a book called, "Change your Story. Change your Life." Abraham Hicks has written several best-selling books about the Law of Attraction. They have done scientific studies that show your words can affect reality. Maseru Emoto did a published experiment about the effect of words on water molecules. He wrote a book about this called "Messages from Water". The book contains photographs of ice crystals after words of both negativity and positivity were spoken while still in water form. The molecular difference was dramatic. The words spoken to these water molecules physically manifested in completely different shapes. If words can affect water crystals, imagine what they can do to our bodies.

Our bodies are composed of 70 percent water. So the words we use to talk to ourselves and how the people closest to us talk to us, affects us on a cellular level. We all have an inner critic. Learning to abate that voice in my head that is constantly telling me that I could have done it better has been a lifelong struggle for me. Dr. Pat Allen, a popular relationship coach in Los Angeles, used to have a business card that read "Don't should on me". In order to recover from my own perfectionism, I have had to take the words, "coulda, woulda, and shoulda" out of my vocabulary. The words "coulda, woulda, and shoulda" are words that are used to beat myself up. These are words of self-doubt. They reinforce the self-destructive belief that I am not good enough. I have also replaced the phrase "I have to" with "I get to". "I have to do something" lowers my vibration and makes it seem like an arduous task. But if "I get to do something", it becomes a privilege. Everything is an "I get to" when you think about it. If you realize how lucky we are just to be alive and living in a human body, you will live in a state of conscious gratitude rather than entitlement.

For example, "I have to go to work today". That feels like work is unbearable and a necessary evil. But if I say, "I get to go to work", that makes work seem like a privilege. When you think about how many people are unemployed and would do anything for a pay check, you realize that going to work is a gift. Same with "I have to go to the gym" versus "I get to go to the gym". Do you know how many people don't have the physical ability to exercise? My father had always been a champion in tennis and ping pong. He wore his knees into the ground by playing tennis well into his seventies. When he was eighty, he got double knee replacement surgery and didn't recover. He spent the last decade of his life struggling to walk. The final two years of his life, he could not walk or even stand without assistance. Right before I got on a treadmill or a spinning bike, I would dedicate my work out to him. He would have done anything to feel the exhilaration of exercise in his body. Why don't you dedicate your workout to the people who don't have the capacity to exercise? It will change your workout. Or thank God that you have a job to support yourself, while so many people live in poverty.

Other defeatist words to take out of your vocabulary are "always" and "never". These words are those of a victim or of blame. For example, "I always have bad luck." Or "I am always a day late and a dollar short". Or blaming another, "You always forget my birthday!" You are not giving them the benefit of the doubt or any room for improvement, "You are always a thorn in my side!" Never isn't much better. For example, "I am never going to fall in love again." Or "I never get promoted at my job". Never is a great word to blame others, "You never send me flowers anymore." Or "You never show up on time!" These words create sweeping generalizations. There is no black and white when it comes to human behavior, life happens in the grey. "Always" and "never" are words of judgement. When we judge ourselves or judge others we are coming from a place of fear and negativity. We want to come from a place of love and uplift ourselves and others with our positivity.

If you can afford a therapist, by all means get one. Having someone you can trust to process your emotions can only help you in life. We all have thought patterns and belief systems that were installed in our childhood. These are default patterns of thinking and behaving. Many of them no longer serve us. Sometimes, we are in our own way and don't even know it. An objective person can help us differentiate the false beliefs from the real. Fear is usually what's blocking us. FEAR stands for False Evidence Appearing Real.

If a therapist is out of your price range, you can try group therapy. Many therapists run groups to reach more clients. Journaling is another great tool. If I can get my scattered thoughts on paper, they become more clear and don't have as much power over me. There's magic and power in the pen. You can also joint a support group. Make sure it is not a support group against something, but for something. What you resist persists. There's a war on almost everything these days. There's a war on drugs, poverty, terrorism, immigrants, homelessness, and police officers. Why can't we be for something instead? We can be for sobriety, for wealth, for peace, for inclusiveness, for rehabilitation of homeless people, and for safe neighborhoods. Find a community that is not about people sitting around playing the victim. I want you to go from victim to VICTOR! There are many great communities around churches, temples, yoga classes and twelve step groups that can help you keep your vibration high.

As much as I value, friends, groups and community, nobody's opinion about you is more important that your own. Wayne Dyer is credited for the famous quote, "What other people think about me is none of my business." In Al Anon they say, "There are three types of business. My Business. Your business. And God's business." All I can control is myself. I am powerless over what others think, say and do. In order to experience the most freedom in life, you can't care what anyone thinks of you. Why are children having so much more fun than adults? It isn't just that they don't have any bills or responsibilities yet. They truly don't care what anybody thinks about them. They are playful and joyful beings. Everything is a game. I like the bumper sticker "Play More. Bark Less". Having fun is such a key component to success. Some of the wealthiest people I know are the most miserable. What is the point in being rich and depressed? Abraham Hicks used to drive around in a huge mobile home that said, "Life is Supposed to be Fun!" We can all learn so much from watching children or dogs play. Life is a game. There are winners, losers, rules, as well as cash and prizes. So if it's a game, we might as enjoy playing it. Stop taking yourself so seriously!

I read on someone's Facebook wall, "If you are single and don't do yoga or have a dog, what are you doing?". It's important to have someone or something to take care of other than yourself. In the movie "28 Days" with Sandra Bullock, when she was leaving her rehab, they told her not to jump into a relationship right away. They said, "If you can take care of a plant, then you can move to a pet. If you can take care of a pet, then you can move into a relationship". I am a huge dog lover. I am on my second Labrador Retriever. The first one Bungalo helped me transition from Florida to L.A. He was there for me when I got sober, when I got engaged, and when I broke it off. He was with me through so many moves and relationships. I took a traveling sales job that allowed him to travel with me to corporate apartments in Oakland, San Jose, and San Diego, California.

He taught me so much! One of the biggest things was how to show up for someone other than myself. I was with him from age eight weeks to his last breath. Oh, what a journey we had! My current Lab, Atticus, has nursed me through my recent divorce and my father's passing. If you don't have the time or the lifestyle to take on the responsibility of being a pet owner, don't do it. But if you can swing it, even if you have to utilize pet walking and pet sitting services, the emotional support you get from a pet is priceless.

If you don't want to take on the responsibility of a dog, a cat is much easier. They are way more independent than dogs. They don't require walks. You just have to feed them and change their litter box. If that is too much, you can help a neighbor with their pet when they have a long day at work or go out of town. Watching animals give love unconditionally and seeing their gratitude for the things we take for granted in life, like food and affection, really help ground you in the present moment. Spending time outside in nature observing animals can also be therapeutic.

AFFIRMATIONS

I AM FEELING MORE PEACEFUL
EVERY DAY.

I ENOY BEING IN THE PRESENT
MOMENT.

I AM ABLE TO PAUSE BEFORE I REACT.

4 ROMANTIC

"Romance is one of the sacred temples that dot the land-scape of life." - Marianne Williamson

In romance, as in business, we attract who we are, not what we want. We all want our dream lover, but have we become our dream person to ourselves? Oscar Wilde said, "To love oneself, is the beginning of a life-long romance." How we feel about ourselves is going to determine the type of relationship we attract. If we talk negatively to ourselves, we are going to attract a lover who talks negatively to us. If we complain all the time, we will find someone else who complains. If we feel unworthy of commitment and have fear of intimacy, we will find someone who won't commit. How we treat ourselves is a mirror for how the world will treat us. So many people are looking to love to fix their emotional pain. And it only creates more emotional pain. Hurt people hurt people. If you are hurting inside, you are going to inadvertently hurt someone else. Isn't that what every sad country western song is about?

Love gone bad. In contrast to most pop songs, romance novels and romantic comedy films, which claim that love is going to fix us and that all our problems will miraculously vanish. No wonder women are spending billions of dollars on beauty treatments and diet products. Because if we could only look prettier, younger, and sexier, we could get a man. That man would solve all our problems. But if you haven't done the inner work and you get into a relationship, eventually the honeymoon phase will pass, and you will still have the same issues. Most people will choose a lover who is like their mother or father so they can work out their unresolved childhood trauma. People choose a mate who is familiar, as in similar to their family. Until they can work through these childhood traumas with a therapist, the 12 Steps, or another type of support group, they will be repeating the same painful patterns that yield the same results.

People wonder how they can change cities, jobs and their looks but still attract the same type of relationship. Those are all outside variables. People have to do the inner work and really understand their base fears and limiting beliefs that are subconsciously driving them. An individual needs to correct their childhood trauma so that they can be so strong that they don't become obsessed with romantic relationships. Like drinking, gambling or shopping, addiction to romance is a real addiction. That is why they have the 12 Step group Sex and Love Addicts Anonymous. Some people will get plastic surgery, move across the world, or go bankrupt to chase romance. Before we can build our fortune, we have to make sure our relationships are life affirming and healthy.

One of the patterns that I have struggled with is seeking lower companions. Nothing makes you feel better about yourself than being with someone who is doing worse. Why do you think celebrity gossip magazines are so popular? We get to read about these rich, gorgeous people going through divorce, rehab, gaining weight, etc. After reading about our favorite star's mental breakdown, we don't feel so bad about ourselves for the rest of the day. But then our negative self-image comes back and we have to buy another gossip magazine. So spending time with a real, live person, whose life is a mess, does the same thing for your self-esteem. I used to think to myself, "I must not have a drinking problem, because I don't drink like he does". Or, "I don't lose my temper, or have credit card debt, or a dirty apartment like he does." So, even though I hate my life, I must be okay. When you are with a lower companion, you feel a sense of superiority and that is a false kind of confidence boost.

Then, I developed a savior complex where I believed that only I could rescue my lower companion from their miserable life. I would bombard him with self-help books, CDs, lectures, seminars, and become his mentor. Most guys are not so attracted to a mentor. They don't want to be taught and preached to by their lover. They are turned off by a mean mother who is constantly pointing out what they did wrong and where they can improve. Healthy men want their girlfriend to admire and respect them. The paradigm of rescuing them is a formula for resentment and animosity. They might appreciate the attention and desire to help in the beginning, but when they get back on their feet, they become bored with the constant nagging. They will often cheat on or leave the mothering girlfriend to find someone who looks up to them, so they can feel better about themselves. That is the typical cliché of the man who cheats on his long-suffering wife with his young assistant, because the assistant appreciates him.

This dynamic is just one example of a toxic relationship, but there are others. Codependency can be very detrimental if you are trying to build wealth. If you are in a relationship with someone who needs to be with you all the time, they are going to drain your energy. A healthy relationship doesn't feel draining or controlling. Find someone who has their own life, so you can have the space to build your dream. Love is space. Even if you are both building the same business together, you can delegate the duties to divide and conquer. Usually, one partner is better behind the scenes with technology, and the other has better communication skills. You both can't be everything to everyone. Find your strengths and have your partner find theirs and delegate. What I believe is a healthier option than a codependent relationship is an interdependent relationship. Both partners have their own full, wonderful life. When they come together and share their life with their beloved, their life get even richer. As the rapper Fabulous said, "I'm a movement by myself, but I'm a force when we're together." Two fully actualized, whole individuals coming together can create a force to be reckoned with.

Another type of toxic relationship is abusive. Putting someone down, name-calling, threatening and punishing are all traits of an abusive relationship. Physical abuse of any kind is uncalled for and should be reported to the authorities. If you want to fly in life, you cannot be bound to someone who is clipping your wings. When I was in an emotionally abusive relationship, I felt like I was running the marathon of life and putting everything I had into winning. But my partner was telling me I looked fat in my running shorts and throwing banana peels at my feet. How could I ever win the race of life with a partner who was constantly sabotaging me? Of course, I couldn't. You are the President of your own life. Your partner is your C.E.O. Would you be able to run a company with a C.E.O. that was constantly insulting you and derailing your company's goals and vision? You know the answer. You couldn't be successful in business. But in this analogy, the "company" is your life. Do you want a life partner who is tearing you down? The logical answer is no. Unfortunately, many people don't use their rational minds when it comes to relationships.

It is amazing to me how many people stay in dysfunctional relationships. They convince themselves that this is the last human being on earth that will ever love them. They fear without this person they will be alone, a fate worse than death. If you break down the word "alone", it is "all" and "one". We are all one! We are never alone. We have your version of God, we have friends, we have community, we have pets. I believe that friends are God's apology for family. Sometimes it is healthier to detach from toxic people, even if they are your family. It is better to be alone than in bad company. If you are alone, you have a blank slate of endless possibilities. But if you are stuck in a dead-end relationship, your world gets really small. You have to find the courage to get out. Feel the fear and do it anyway. Your quality of life depends on it. How many people have wasted their life being in a miserable relationship with the wrong person? If you knew a positive, motivated, like-minded soul was out there, not only for you, but looking for you, would you have the strength to leave? One of my favorite relationship coaches, Allison Armstrong, said, "There is no scarcity of people. You don't have a finding problem. You have a sorting problem. How fast can you sort?"

With internet dating apps, it makes the sorting process even faster and more entertaining. The most important thing to look for is someone who has a complementary lifestyle. If you are sober, you might want to stay away from a heavy drinker. If you are health conscious, you won't be happy with an overweight smoker. If you are spiritual, an atheist is not going to be a good fit. They should also have similar long term goals. Your love interest might really want to raise a family, but maybe you want to travel the world. These are the questions to ask during the dating process.

Everyone laments about how hard dating is, but it is a necessary evil. How else are you going to surmise that you are on the same page? If your goal is to build an empire, you might want to stay away from a starving artist, who thinks money is the root of all evil. I am not saying that you have to date your clone. All people are unique and have their own quirks. Maybe you love to sleep in on the weekends, but your significant other wants to wake up at 5 am and walk on the beach with you. If it is not a major issue, then you can compromise and wake up an hour earlier than usual to walk on the beach. I am talking about major issues like health, family, travel, spirituality, and finances. Life is challenging enough on its own, so find someone who has a complementary world view. You want someone who will enhance your life, not detract from it. If they make your life harder, what is the point?

If you are reading this book, you are probably purpose-driven. You have goals and dreams. Many people are not that motivated. They work a job. Job is spelled J.O.B., which stands for just, over, broke. They pay you just enough money to pay your bills, but not enough money to actually enjoy your life. If you are with someone who is happy if they just pay their bills on time, and has no drive to make anything more of their life, it is not going to be a fit. That is why it is so important to wait to have sex. Once you have sex with someone, you are bonded. It is so easy to overlook their values, habits, and life outlook. I know so many people these days are having casual sex. Many have come to expect it within the first three dates. But how can you really get to know someone that quickly? I have been in relationships with many guys that were not right for me, because I jumped

31

into bed with them. I know when the chemistry runs high, it is tempting to be intimate right away.

How much time do you want to waste with someone who does not serve you and what you want out of life? I don't believe in neutral energy. People are either adding value and making your life better or they are detracting from your life and making it worse. Aren't you worth someone who makes your life even better?

Wouldn't it feel amazing to be part of a power couple? The sum can be greater than the individual parts.

If you were building a home that you intended to reside in for the rest of your life, you would hire an architect. You would tell him exactly what you wanted. Then he would come up with a blueprint. Why do we put more thought into planning a vacation than we do into what we want in a life partner? Maybe we think that it is more romantic to be at the whim of fate when it comes to matters of the heart. I advise the contrary. The Universe responds when we are specific. If you say, "I want a relationship", you will most likely get a relationship. But will it be a healthy relationship that makes you happy? You are rolling the dice. The majority of people that are in relationships are not happy. I encourage you not to settle for anything that is thrown your way. But instead to be clear about what you want by writing it down. Make a list of all the characteristics you want in your ideal mate. Their looks, education, success level, but most importantly how do you feel when you are with them. That is the bottom line of why we want to get into a romantic relationship. We want to feel a certain way.

Once you get your list of who you want to attract and how you want to feel, you have another assignment; to become the person on your list. You are who you hang around with. If you want to attract a smart, funny and successful person, then you need to work on those traits in yourself. If you want a partner who makes you feel authentic, playful and sexy, then you need to do things that cultivate those feelings. When you feel so confident and happy with your life that you don't even care about being in a relationship is exactly when that person is going to show up.

People are turned off by other's neediness. When you are desperate to be in a relationship, you scare people away without even realizing it. Most communication is subconscious. But if you are loving life, without being in a relationship, people are going to be drawn to you and not even know why. You will magnetize people to you because they like being around your positive energy. You don't need to wait to be ready for a relationship. You don't need to be a certain age, dress size or have wealth. You just have to fall in love with your life. When you are genuinely enjoying life, people will be drawn to you like moths to a light.

AFFIRMATIONS

I AM MAGICALLY, PASSIONATELY
IN LOVE WITH MY SOUL MATE.

I HAVE A HEALTHY, LOVING,
COMMITTED RELATIONSHIP.

I AM ABLE TO BE A LOVING PRESENCE
IN THE WORLD.

5 MENTAL

"There are no great limits to growth because there are no limits of human intelligence, imagination and wonder."
- Ronald Reagan

Your attitude is everything in life. You are either having positive thoughts or negative thoughts. There is no such thing as a neutral thought. Your thoughts become your beliefs. Your beliefs become your attitude. Your attitude becomes your energy. Your energy becomes your vibration. A positive vibration magnetizes positive experiences such as love, abundance, health, vitality and joy. A negative vibration repels all these good experiences and attracts negative experiences. Your word is the advertisement that you are sending to the boundaries of the Universe. Be very mindful of what you say. But it is more than just your words. How many times have we said affirmations over and over again but our results don't change? That is because we don't believe the affirmation will come true. We are just paying lip service in hopes it might come true. You have to visualize and experience how you will feel when your manifestation comes true. How will you feel walking into your dream home? How do you feel in the arms of your beloved?

People are either enhancing your vibration or detracting from it. Have you ever spent time with someone who was constantly worrying or complaining? I have, and I felt incredibly drained afterwards. Many people who are on a path of personal growth come from families that are negative. When you visit with them, I encourage you to limit your time with them and have plenty of alone time. When traveling to visit family, if you can afford it, rent a hotel room and a car. If you must spend time with them, continue your self-care by eating healthy, getting a good night's sleep and exercising. Ram Das, a spiritual teacher, writer, and psychologist, said it best; "If you think you are enlightened, go spend a week with your family." I have also heard that fish and family both go bad after three days. We can't change our family. But we can certainly protect ourselves from their negativity. I like the saying that friends are God's apology for family.

Many times, your old friends and family will attempt to convince you to get off your spiritual path. They will say that they liked you better when you were depressed. Again, as the saying goes, "misery loves company". If you stay negative, they don't have to look at themselves. But if you come home happy, they realize how unhappy they are. The last thing a person who is upset wants to see is someone who is happy, smiling, bright eyed and bushy-tailed. They don't want you to teach and preach that they can change their reality by changing their thoughts. They don't care. They just want everyone to stay down in the dumps with them. Most people don't realize that we can actually choose our own thoughts. Your mind is like a finely-tuned radio. If you have a negative thought, you can change your focus to a positive thought.

A great tool to change your focus is gratitude. Many people keep a gratitude journal and write lists of everything going well in their lives. The more gratitude you have the more the Universe will give you to be grateful for. Gratitude is a great tool for manifestation. Gratitude is an attitude. You can always pick any person or situation apart and focus on what's wrong about it. It takes mental discipline and training to focus on what is right about it. Reverend Michael Beckwith talks of the need "to find the message in the mess". Every situation can be a learning experience. I do a journal where I ask myself, "how is the worst thing that happened to me today actually the best thing?" I don't know what's best for me. I think I do, but I really don't. How many situations have seemed awful at the time, but in retrospect you learned unique lessons, that you could not have learned in any other way?

A big part of being on a spiritual path is to have the humility of not knowing. I think I know what's best for me, but I have to have the humility to say I don't know. There have been relationships, jobs, vacations that I thought would be the answer to all of my issues, but they weren't. I like the saying "rejection is God's protection". I have to believe that things don't work out for a reason. There were certain relationships that I forced or pursued when I knew they did not serve me and they caused a lot of pain. It is so much easier to live in the vortex of surrender and believe that I don't have to force or push anything. If something is meant for me, nothing or no one can stop it. And if something is not meant for me, no matter how much energy I push around, it will not happen for me. Or if it does, it will be to my detriment. How much energy have we wasted trying to force results? I believe in taking action, but leaving the results up to God. And trusting that whatever happens is God's will for me.

There are other tools to help you develop and stay in a positive mindset. YouTube has thousands of teachers, mentors, seminars, Ted talks, talk shows, and interviews that can inspire you to keep your attitude positive. There are seminars you can take in person, books to read, meet ups, 12 Step meetings, churches, temples, yoga classes and many other avenues to stay positive. Your vibe attracts your tribe. When you shift your vibration, you will become an attraction to other positive-minded people. This will be a relief because there is usually a detoxification process, where your old friends will go away. As painful as it might feel to lose dear friends, they are simply no longer a vibrational match. Nature abhors a void. Hang tight and you will soon meet new, more positive like-minded friends. We can't choose our family, but we can choose our friends. You might be asking yourself, where will you find these new friends?

You can join a book club, a meditation class, go on a retreat. The consciousness movement is so prevalent in our culture that there will be events that will resonate with you. As important as it is not to have extensive conversations and spend time with negative people, you also don't want to watch television or movies with negative content. When we are being entertained, all of our defenses are down. The violence, misogyny, racism, and lowest common denominator values that are so prevalent in our society are also portrayed in the media. I only watch content that has a humorous or uplifting message. There are plenty of comedies, romances, and 'triumph of the human spirit' stories to enjoy. Why burden your system with dark, negative messages? Your body doesn't know the difference between reality, your thoughts, or what you see on the screen. The adrenaline and the cortisol that gets released in your body is the same as if you were experiencing what you are watching in real time.

It goes without saying to avoid watching the news on television. There is a saying in journalism, "If it bleeds, it leads".

Not only does the news focus on incredibly negative and scary stories, it embellishes them with imagery and music. If everyone believed everything they saw on the news, they would be smart to never leave their house. The news portrays danger lurking around every corner, every food and product can be fatal, too. Usually the morning news has more positive stories about beneficial diets, exercises and more inspirational stories.

What you watch right before you go to bed affects your subconscious the most. So watching the evening news with all its gloom and doom is the worst thing you could do, if you want to program your mind to think positively. Utilize this powerful time to change your attitude for the better. You can watch a funny show, listen to a powerful speaker on YouTube, read a book, or write in your journal. Many people end their day with a gratitude journal.

In contrast, that is why visualization is so powerful. There have been numerous studies with athletes who dramatically enhances their performance by visualizing their success in their respective sport. Why not spend a few minutes each day visualizing what you want to experience in your life? Be it with your health, romance or finances, your visualization can help you achieve your dreams. For those who don't like to visualize, try writing down your goals, using affirmations or making a vision board. You can use the phone app Pinterest to create a digital vision board to manifest the life you want. You can have a board for all the areas discussed in this book. When you are bored waiting in line at the grocery store, add some images to your vision board.

You can also use the phone app Instagram to follow people that inspire you. These images are going into your subconscious and are quite powerful. There are people who post fashion, fitness, business, and travel images. When we go on a journey, we are more motivated if we know our destination. Imagine just driving your car around aimlessly; it might be relaxing, depending on traffic. But driving to a vacation destination, a party or a concert is a lot more enlivening. If soccer or football didn't have a goal, the sport would be boring to watch. Going for a goal makes life exciting! Life is a game. If you want to make it count, know what you want, and enjoy the adventure of manifesting your goal. If you can believe it, you can achieve it. The first person to convince that you are worthy of your goals is yourself. You can do all the right things, but if deep down in your soul, you don't believe it can happen to you, it won't. Whatever you believe about yourself, you're right. If you think you are a loser that is destined for misery and poverty, you're right. If you think you are a leader that can be successful and happy, you are right.

There's something that is usually referenced in sports called "mental toughness". But when you are on a path of transformation, it also applies. You have to make a decision to keep your vibration high and stay positive no matter what. There are certain people, usually someone close to you, that want to bring you down. They are the most challenging to stay positive with because they know all the buttons to push. The joke is that your parents, especially, know how to push your buttons, because they installed them. What I like to do is to play a game in my head. I know going into the situation with them that they will be attempting to get my goat and to bring me down. So I set the intention of staying positive. It's like playing tennis. When they say something negative, I don't react but retort with something positive. It is truly a test of wills. Many times I have failed playing this game and I get snagged by their insults. But, when I can stay on my game and return their snide comments with loving remarks, it is fun to see how frustrated they get. Of course, the goal is not to get them upset. On the contrary, the point is to stay positive, but certain people get a false sense of power by getting people to react. If you don't react, you win.

AFFIRMATIONS

I AM READING OR LISTENING TO
SOMETHING EVERY DAY THAT
INSPIRES ME.

I HAVE FIVE MINUTES A DAY TO SIT
STILL AND QUIET MY MIND.

I AM ABLE TO LEARN SOMETHING
FROM EVERYONE WHO CROSSES
MY PATH.

6 Social

"You can discover more about a person in an hour of play, than in a year of conversation." - Plato

On the path to success, who you hang around is crucial. In fact, you are who you hang around with. There's a saying, "Birds of a feather, flock together." Most people's attitudes, health, happiness and finances are exactly like their friends' and family's. Most people are fear-based and negative in their thinking. If someone tries to change their situation for the better, it is human nature for them to try to bring them back down to the status quo. There are even families and subcultures where it is considered not cool to achieve, to work hard, or to be a success. That is an average person, job mentality. As we have learnt already in this book, J.O.B. stands for Just, Over, Broke. They pay you just enough money to get by and get your bills paid, but not enough money to get rich. I remember being in high school and down-playing how much I studied or that I had got an "A" on my test, so I would fit in. In real life, your report card is your paycheck. It is time to stop caring what others think and go for it! If someone isn't going to pay your bills and give you enough money to retire, then who cares what they think. We are born alone and we die alone. The only opinion that matters is how you think of yourself.

Your friends are either giving you positive energy and supporting your growth and unfolding, or they are bringing you down. There is no such thing as neutral energy. They are enhancing or detracting from your well-being. How you feel when you walk away from them is a good clue. When I walk away from positive people I feel happy and energized. When I walk away from negative people, I just want to go home and sleep. When I know I am going to be spending time with negative people, I mentally surround myself with white light and I do my best to detach. There are certain people who will deliberately want to snag you by pushing your buttons, challenging you or even being rude. I think of it like a game. I know their goal is to get me to react, but my goal is to stay positive and deflect their negativity. When someone is trying to provoke you, don't react. I heard in a 12 Step meeting, to not J.A.D.E. Don't Justify, Argue, Defend or Explain. If I lower my vibration, and argue with them, then they win. As Abraham Hicks says, "Nothing is more important than feeling good."

Let's talk about the "J" in J.A.D.E. Don't justify. I used to think that I was a human 'doing', not a human 'being'. I did not feel lovable just because I existed. I felt that I had to earn love from people. I always felt that I wasn't enough. I was constantly feeling the need to prove myself by wanting to do more, be more, and have more. I was a people-pleaser. I felt like I had to get people to like me and approve of me, just to feel okay about myself. But it was impossible to get everyone to like me. If I went to a party and 99 out of a 100 people there told me I looked great and loved my dress, I would focus on the one person who didn't. I would wonder, "why didn't he say he liked my dress? What's wrong with me?"

I used to dress for other people, now I just dress for myself. Clothes are a vehicle for creative, self-expression for me. And now, when I go to a social function, I am not trying to see what I can take from it, but how I can contribute. That applies to life, as well. I already have everything I need. My job is to be of service to the world and share my gifts, rather than take from the world. People can smell neediness and desperation. Healthy relationships, both business and personal, are about partnership.

The "A" in J.A.D.E. stands for argue. Have you ever noticed that nobody really wins an argument. Everyone perceives the world through their own lens. It is very challenging to get someone to actually shift their perception. Discussing is different than arguing. Discussion is more of an interchange of ideas for the purpose of learning. Both parties are freely able to share their point of view and to discuss the similarities and the variants. But an argument has a winner and a loser. Who wants to waste their energy winning? As I asked in a previous chapter, "Do you want to be right, or happy?" There are certain phrases you can say to diffuse an avid arguer, such as, "You could be right; That's an interesting point; I will have to consider that; Let me think about that; Can I get back to you on that? You make a great point; If I were you, I would feel the same way; I understand." For some people, this technique will upset them, because they actually enjoy arguing. They like the negative attention and it makes them feel alive. When you refuse to participate in their game, you win the argument and keep your vibration high.

The "D" in J.A.D.E. stands for defend. I used to think if someone accused me of something, I would have to defend myself and prove to them I was innocent. Now I don't care what they think of me. The book "A Course in Miracles" says, "If I defend myself, I am attacked." So that means if I don't bite the hook and defend myself, then the attack doesn't work. It's like Jesus said in the Bible, "Do not resist an evil person; but whoever slaps you on your right cheek, turn the other to him also." In fact, do not resist anything you don't want. What you resist, persists. Some people only know how to connect through attacking. They are full of fear and are crying out for love. If they attack and you only give them back love, they will either go away or they will let down their guard and receive your love. Love is always stronger than fear. Love will always win. Martin Luther King said, "Darkness cannot drive out darkness; only light can do that. Hate cannot drive out hate; only love can do that."

The "E" in J.A.D.E. stands for explain. I don't need to explain myself or my actions. The most important step in living a fully actualized life is to be authentic. In this society, where consumerism tells us to dress a certain way, look a certain way, act a certain way and smell a certain way, being authentic is not highly sought after. But the icons, the people who make the biggest difference in the world, are people who have mastered the art of being their authentic self. People who can be their authentic selves are the most free. What more do we want in life than freedom? Social freedom, financial freedom, freedom of speech, and freedom to explore the world are the most important aspects of living my best life. If I am always explaining myself, then I am diminishing my freedom.

Another thing that blocks one's authenticity is drugs and alcohol. Now people can argue that drugs and alcohol make you feel less inhibited and more free, but to me that is a crutch. They say alcohol gives you confidence and it is even called liquid courage. But it is a false confidence. Being dependent on a substance in any form, liquid, powder, leaf or vapor is not freedom, but imprisonment. In my opinion, these substances block my connection to Source energy. I want to feel my feelings, absorb ideas, see the signs that the Universe is sending me. When I am under the influence, it dulls my senses. Almost all crime, murder, fighting, and fatal car accidents involve alcohol and drugs. If you want to change your life and are addicted to any substance, I would highly recommend getting sober. There are literally thousands of rehabs, treatment centers, outpatient and inpatient detox centers to help you. There are therapists that specialize in substance abuse and of course, Alcoholics Anonymous meetings for continued sobriety and support. If you want to get wealthy, the amount of time, energy and money you will save by getting sober will astound you.

If you can just have a drink and it doesn't affect your mood or your life in any way, I am not talking about you. Only you can decide if alcohol and drugs are a detrimental force in your life. Usually partiers hang out with other partiers. If you are looking to change your current lifestyle to a healthier one, being friends with other sober people is important, especially in the beginning, when you are just getting used to being sober. In fact, whatever journey you are on, being in fellowship with like-minded people is crucial. You are going to enjoy sharing your victories and triumphs with people who understand what you are trying to overcome, both personally and financially. As the saying goes, "Your vibe attracts your tribe"! When I first quit drinking, I didn't think that anything would be fun sober, from dancing, to parties, sex, or even vacation. It is actually more fun sober!

Vacationing is actually an important part of being successful. When we are on the path to wealth and success, we need to reward ourselves with milestones. I can push myself hard for 90 days, if I tell myself I will have a vacation. But if I toil endlessly with no goal in sight, I can get discouraged and burnt out. If the money is tight, it doesn't have to be an exotic vacation, it can be a 'staycation' in your own city. I remember going to the Hard Rock Hotel in Singapore, and I was shocked that almost everyone staying in the hotel was actually from Singapore. There are nice hotels in your own town, where you can leave the kids with a babysitter or take them with you. It's amazing what a couple nights away from your regular routine can do to boost your mood. Or, if you don't even have the money for a hotel, you can take a day trip. Pick a location a couple hours away from where you reside and explore. Have an adventure! It can be a museum, a zoo, a hike, or any historical point of interest. Your mini-vacay can be visiting an old friend who moved outside of town. It really doesn't matter what it is, as long as you have a break in your routine to look forward to.

You can even reward yourself short-term as a motivation. Sometimes, when I don't feel like going to the gym, I will tell myself that if I work out, I can get a fancy juice or tea drink. Whatever it takes to motivate yourself. If you have a big week at work, you can treat yourself to a massage or a trip to the spa. Another way to reward yourself is to spend time with your friends. I believe that women need girl time and men need guy time. If you spend every second with your significant other, you can get bored and the relationship can lose its luster. When women are with women and men are with men, they can let loose and communicate in a different kind of way. When we are with the opposite sex, there's always an aspect of performing or being on your game. But when you are with your same sex in a social setting, you can take some time off from people pleasing, and really relax. I love that part of the Korean culture is that the women go to the spa several times a week. They spend hours talking to each other and pampering themselves by soaking in the jacuzzi, saunas, steam rooms, massages, and even just watching television. In the Korean spas, the men and the women are separated. Many men bond over poker, golf, bowling and other sports. It's important when you are in a new relationship to not abandon your friends. Life is about balance.

Now that you have found your life-enhancing friends, don't be shy about planning fun things to do. There are daily emails and social networking lists you can get on that will tell you the exciting events that are happening in your city. Most people are stuck in their routine, like a hamster on the treadmill. You can help them break that monotony by inviting them to fun events. You are being a leader by taking the initiative. Not everyone is as open-minded or has the time or money to participate in your plan. So don't take it personally when someone says "no". Chances are it has nothing to do with you. If you can't find anyone to go with you, you can always go by yourself. You will be able to come and go as you wish. You will meet more people when you are alone because it forces you to strike up a conversation with someone new. How many times have I gone to a party and just talked to my friend who I talk to every day, rather than meeting someone new. If you don't know how to open a conversation with someone who looks interesting to you, simply extend your hand and say, "Hi. My name is... How are you today?" Now the conversation is off the ground.

I used to feel that when I was socializing, I was losing time and money, because I was not focusing on my work. But playing actually enhances my work. In sales, you end up saying the same thing, your pitch, a million times. If you are bored of saying it, your customers are going to feel it. Mixing up your work with playing will give you renewed passion. Your clients will sense your enthusiasm for life. Emotions are contagious. If you can get your customers excited, they are more likely to buy your product. Networking is also an important aspect of socializing. Every industry has networking mixers and events. These events are great because you can make new friends that are also goal-oriented and ambitious.

You can get clients, give clients, brainstorm. Even if the person you meet at the event is not interested in your business, they might know someone who is. You want to be an owl to be successful in business, "Who, who, who, who do you know, that I can talk to about my product?" Everyone is connected to everyone, especially in this internet-based, social media-driven world. The difference between an average sales person and a successful one, is their ability to garner referrals. Word of mouth has always been the best and the most sincere form of advertising.

There's two types of marketing. Cold market is selling to people you have never met. It is extremely challenging to sell to strangers. You have to do huge volumes of cold calls to get sales, because there is absolutely no trust. You are simply relying on the law of averages to eventually call enough people to find someone who is seeking your product. It can be very costly and time-consuming to do business this way. But with warm market, everyone knows each other. It is more fun and easier to sell to people you know or who your clients know. They are already friends and family so there is a higher degree of trust there. People will buy from you if they like you and trust you. With warm market they automatically like and trust you based on their friend's recommendation. So give your customers incentives for referring you to their warm market. You can offer prizes, freebies, gift cards or services, if they give you some referrals. The difference between average business people and top producers is their ability to get referrals. Don't be shy about asking for referrals. You will be amazed that when people believe in your product, they are more than happy to spread the word. In business you are getting paid to make friends with everyone. Treat all your customers as your friends, because they are!

AFFIRMATIONS

I AM SURROUNDED BY PEOPLE WHO
LOVE AND SUPPORT ME.

I HAVE FUN AND PLAY WITH PEOPLE
WHO LIFT ME UP.

I AM ABLE TO SPEND TIME WITH
PEOPLE WHO ARE POSITIVE AND
ABUNDANT.

7 FINANCIAL

"The standard of success in life is not the things or the money. The standard for success in life is absolutely the amount of joy you feel." - Abraham Hicks

As the quote above explains, happy is the new rich! How many wealthy people do you know that are completely miserable? How many wealthy people do you know that are mentally or physically unhealthy? You can have all the money in the world, but if you don't have the mental or physical capacity to enjoy it, then what is it really worth? You can't take it with you when you die. The point of attaining wealth is to experience joy while you are here. Joy comes from freedom. Money gives you true freedom. The freedom to do what you want, when you want, where you want, and with who you want. The reason why finances are the last chapter in the book, even though this is a book on abundance, is that money is the last piece of the puzzle. If you don't have your health, your relationships, your support group, and your mental attitude right, the money won't come. If you do have those areas functioning at peak capacity, the money has to come.

Abraham Hicks who is quoted above and one of my favorite spiritual teachers says that everyone always asks, "What is my purpose? How do I find my path?" I love their answer. They say that "your path will find you." If you are living your best life, you will attract the right people, places, things and situations to get you to your next step. You don't have to figure out your whole life. That is overwhelming and anxiety-provoking. All you have to do is take the next indicated action. If you are listening to that still, small voice which is always communicating with you, and being receptive to the signs the Universe is sending you, your next step will be obvious. It usually comes from listening to others and being present in the moment. You never know who God is going to use to point you in the right direction. I am stubborn, so unless I hear the same message several times from several people, I won't listen. It could be to meditate more, to read a certain book, take a seminar, or see a movie. But whatever that next step is, it will get your soul to the next level of personal growth.

If you are not sure what avenue to pursue to attain wealth, ask yourself some pertinent questions.

- Why do you want money?
- If you won the lottery and never had to work, what would you do?
- When are you the happiest?
- Who do you want to provide for?
- What are you excited to give?
- What do you want to contribute to the world?
- What do you want your legacy to be?
- What is your life purpose?

I suggest you get out a pen and paper and just write down the answers to the above questions without judging yourself. You will be surprised by what you really want. So many of us are programmed to want what our society or parents want for us. You are not your parental fantasy. My parents wanted me to be a doctor or lawyer or marry one. I did neither and I have never been happier. I like the movie "The Dead Poet's Society". One of the characters wanted to be an actor, but his father had other plans for him. He committed suicide because he knew he could never be happy living out his life as planned by his father. No need for such extremes, but isn't it time you stopped living your life for others and figured out what makes you tick? It's called finding your "why". Your "why" will get you out of bed when you would rather sleep in. Your "why" will keep you showing up when you want to throw in the towel. Just get up, suit up and show up; and you will be amazed what will happen. 85% of success is simply showing up. So many people quit when they are so close to attaining wealth. As the saying goes, "Don't quit five minutes before the miracle".

A big part of having a balanced life, as you strive for your goal, is time-management. I use time blocking for everything. Meditation, working out, taking care of my dog, socializing and especially working. If I give myself a time limit, I can handle anything. I need to know my activity has a beginning and an end. I enjoy circuit training because I know I can push myself on the treadmill or on a weight station for a set amount of time. In other words, I know when the torture will end. The same applies to business. Tell yourself that you are going to make prospect calls for the next hour. However many appointments you yield is beyond your control. But you can work the phone for an hour. Due to the law of averages, you will automatically get a certain number of appointments. When you do time blocking, you are not diffusing your awareness. Women, especially, are natural multitaskers and can do several activities at once. In time blocking, you pick one activity, and give all of your attention to it. Whether its social time or time at the office, know what area of life you are participating in and don't hold back. That's where the saying "work hard, play hard" comes from.

If having a balanced lifestyle appeals to you, I strongly suggest owning your own business or going into all commission sales. If you are working forty hours a week, doing time blocking is a lot more difficult because your time belongs to your employer. You can certainly switch your focus during the hours you are at the office, to attain goals and achieve tasks. But to experience the joy and freedom I am talking about it helps to control your own schedule. When you have control over your own calendar, setting yourself up for success is crucial. I recommend taking some time to sit down on Sunday to plan out your week. In setting up your schedule, make sure to set aside several focus days and a play day. On your focus days you are condensing a 40 hour work week into an 8-10 hour day. On these days you will do the heavy lifting aspects of your business. The cold calling, appointment setting, follow up emails, customer servicing, and of course the sales meetings with prospects. On your play day, don't look at your phone or respond to business related emails. Really find something you enjoy doing. It could be a hike, playing your favorite sport, going to a museum, shopping or anything that makes your heart sing! You will return to your next focus day with renewed determination and vigor. And you will be ready to play the ultimate game, the law of averages.

In sales, and in business generally, it is all a numbers game. So many leads, result in so many calls, result in so many appointments, which result in so many closes. The whole sales cycle stems from the leads. If you don't have the leads, you don't have the prospects and you have nobody to share your business with. In your own business, it is of paramount importance to invest in leads. Without the capital for marketing, you really have no income stream. No matter how wonderful your product is, it can't sell itself. I have had many people ask me to go into business with them. My first question is always, "Where are you going to get your leads?" Because without leads, you have no business.

Another reason to be in commission sales is that you have all the freedom of owning your own business, with none of the liability. When you own a business you are responsible for inventory, marketing, paying rent, payroll, taxes, and insurance among many other things. But if you are a sales person, someone else is putting themselves on the line. All you have to do is apply your time, energy and talent. Network marketing is one of the most challenging sales careers one might have. Many people have failed, yet more millionaires are created from network marketing than any other industry in America. If you have minimal money to invest and are willing to work hard, you can have all the perks of owning a business with minimal overhead. The most important aspect of any sale, is that you believe in what you are selling. You have to be a product of your product. If you are selling cars, you should drive the car you are selling. If you are selling nutritional supplements, you should be taking them yourself. If you are selling real estate, you should own or have the goal of owning property. If you are currently selling a product that you don't believe in, you are out of integrity. You will never hit your maximum earning capacity if you don't believe what you are saying. People can smell insincerity.

In sales, you want to master your pitch. A great sales pitch is like a great monologue, it should evoke emotion in your client. People buy on emotion, not on logic. People are more impressed by the height of your enthusiasm, than the depth of your knowledge. Emotions are contagious. If you are excited about your product, your prospect is going to feed off your excitement. Many sales people bore their prospects by flooding them with detailed information about the product. Only a small percentage of our population is motivated by details. Most people just want to know before they buy something the following: "This is simple. It works. I can do it." When you bombard people with too much data, they get confused. You want to build confidence in your customers, not confusion. You want them to walk away thinking "I got this!" The best way to sell a product is to sample it. Why do you think Costco has so many samples? A great product will sell itself. If you are not selling a consumable product, let your client experience it firsthand. Let them drive the car, or go through a software demo.

A good sales pitch will also overcome every objection to buying. The two most common objections are time and money. It is your job it create so much value in your product that people want to invest their time and money. People in this fast-paced era have less time than ever. Technology was intended to automate simple activities to give us more time for the important aspects of life. It backfired. We are moving so quickly through life, that we have less time than ever before. Between earning a living, childcare, fitness and maintaining a home, our time is spread thin. In order to convince someone to invest time in your product or service, they better have a huge pay off. That is your job as a salesperson to relay. Your goal is to raise the value of your product so high, that people will find the time to invest.

People are just as careful with their money. We are working harder than ever but the cost of living is also higher than ever. In the state of California, the average home costs

$500,000. How can an average person afford a mortgage on a half a million dollar home? They can't. Most people live pay check to pay check. They are ninety days away from total bankruptcy, if they stop working. So it would make sense that they are careful with how they spend their money. In a good sales pitch, you make them want to spend their money because they see the value. How do you create value? You create it through stories. 'Facts tell and stories sell' was taught to me by one of my sales mentors, Bill Gouldd.

Testimonials are a crucial part of any sales pitch. It is a scientific fact that people can feel happiness by watching someone else feel happy. If you are sharing success stories of other customers, who have had a positive experience with your product, they are going to feel that positive emotion. If you can get someone to feel something positive, they buy. You want to stay away from negative words or imagery. Don't mention cancelling or anyone your product did not work for. If they ask you questions, answer honestly, but dwell on the positive aspects of who your product worked for and how it made a difference in their lives.

No matter how great your sales pitch is, before anyone will buy anything from you, they have to like you and trust you. How do you build credibility with a new client? You have to be your best self. Look your best. Take the time to dress the part. Every industry has its own culture. How you would dress to sell private jets is different than how you dress to sell a tractor. Know your clientèle and dress like them, but a little more 'put together'. If you are just starting out and can't afford the right clothes, ask your friends for clothes they are no longer wearing or go to a thrift shop. You might be amazed by what you can find in a second-hand store, if you have the patience to sort through the clothing. When I first started in sales, I was right out of college and didn't know how to dress. I wore Timberland boots with a hoodie and a trench coat to my first sales seminar, I looked like I was going to a hip hop party. My first mentor, Gregg Amerman, pulled me aside and told me to go shopping with one of the top female producers in the company. She took me shopping for beautiful business suits. I wore those for years, but when I came to Los Angeles, those suits were too dressy. The style in California is business casual. I hired a wardrobe stylist, Jennifer Butler, to pick which colors and styles best suited me. She was worth every dime because my clients could see me and hear me when I was dressed as my authentic self.

Being the best you can be also means leaving all your problems at the door. Everyone has problems. The only people who don't have problems are dead. But your problems have no place in a sales meeting. Don't make your prospects or your co-workers your therapist. Leave your problems in the car. That is why your car has locks. You can lock your problems in your car theoretically, so they can't follow you into the office. People can feel your energy. If you are upset, even if you are giving your best sales pitch, your negativity will repel the customers before they can buy from you.

The best way to build rapport with your clients is to find similarities between them and you. Find out about what they like, their hobbies, where they have traveled, their neighborhood, to create some 'me too's'. They are from Italy, you love Italian food. If they are wearing Nike shoes, you too love Nike shoes. If they are from back east, you went to school back east. People will trust you more when they realize you are just like them. It is human nature to be wary of those who are different than us. I have rushed through some of my sales pitches and skipped the vital step of building rapport, and even though the customers bought from me that day, they would later cancel on me.

Some customers go home and tell their friends and neighbors what they bought, and the well-meaning friend tells them they made a mistake. The customer feels embarrassed and humiliated by making a wrong decision. Because you didn't take the time to build trust, they feel scammed. That is the worst feeling as a sales person, to have a client cancel because they don't trust you. When one of their friends or family members challenges their decision to buy from you, you want them armed with documentation. You want them to know exactly what they bought and why. Sending them home with promotional materials is crucial. That way the skeptical friend can read up on what they purchased and not "neg out" your customer.

Giving people sincere compliments and saying their name, as described in the oldie but goodie book "How to Win Friends and Influence People", are also fast ways to build rapport. Making eye contact and really listening are important. People are so accustomed to staring at machines all day, they feel special when someone truly connects with them. Embody the namaste consciousness, the God in you salutes and acknowledges the God in them. Not many people carry the love vibration. If you are treating everyone as the son or daughter of the Most High, they will feel comfortable with you. Don't just try to close a sale, open a relationship. If your customers sense you are just looking for a close, they won't trust you. If you are taking a genuine interest in them and making a friend, they will relax. Building relationships is the key to any successful business. You don't just want a one-time sale, you want a repeat customer. Better yet, you want your customers to like you so much, they give you referrals. The best prospects are friends and family, because you don't have to work so hard to establish trust. The trust is already there from the person who referred them to you.

You attract who you are, not who you want. This bodes true in relationships as well as in business. The Law of Attraction says that which is likened to itself is drawn. So you have to be your best self in all areas. If you follow the different categories in this book, you will be putting your best self forward in the cornerstones of your life experience. I used to only feel comfortable with financially-challenged clients. The wealthier the client was, the more intimidated I felt. Of course, on a spiritual level, I know that we are all exactly the same in God's eyes. But for some reason, I felt that if a client was more successful than me, they had the upper hand. I had to treat them the same as any other client, but I also realized that they were used to calling the shots. I couldn't bully them or use transparent sales techniques to get them to buy. I just had to present all the information and give them an incentive to buy. For example, I could give them a special discount or a payment plan, to create urgency. But if they still didn't close, I had to graciously give them time to think about it.

Don't pressure people to do anything. Every time you meet with a client, it is like going on a date. Romantic relationships take time. One night stands do not. Don't go for the close in the first sales meeting. Build the relationship and show the value of your goods or service. People in this day and age are turned off by pushy sales people. Everyone has heard every traditional pitch and gimmick. Don't act as a sales person, but as a concerned friend. Offer solutions and let your prospect choose which solution best suits their needs. Don't ask a "yes" or "no" question. Don't ask them what they think.

Simply ask them alternative questions. "Do you want to buy A or B?" Don't ask them "if" they are going to buy. You have got to assume the sale. If they didn't want to buy, why would they have taken the time to meet with you? They are going to buy something from someone even if it's not you. Multiple questions are how we have been trained to think by our educational system. Remember all those "true" and "false" tests and multiple choice questions. Have your pitch include multiple choice questions which are all in your favor. Say, "Do you want option A, B, or C?" Don't say, "So are you going to buy this product from me?" Or even worse don't ask, "So what do you think?" An open-ended question gives them total control. When you offer multiple choice closing question, you remain in the driver's seat.

Most importantly, be confident. If you are nervous, act as if you are totally sure of yourself. Emanate the belief that they are buying from you because you are the best sales person with the best product.

AFFIRMATIONS

I AM MAKING A SIX FIGURE INCOME
WORKING PART-TIME.

I HAVE A BEAUTIFUL, BALANCED,
ABUNDANT LIFE.

I AM ABLE TO HAVE THE FREEDOM
TO DO WHAT I WANT, WHEN I WANT,
WHERE I WANT AND WITH WHO I
WANT.

CONCLUSION

"Success is nothing more than a few simple disciplines practiced every day." - Jim Rohn

The people who have achieved the greatest victories in life have had a coach. Halle Berry thanked her acting coach Ivanna Chubbuck in her Oscar acceptance speech. Michael Jordan, one of the best basketball players and greatest athletes of all time, had a coach. Nobody has to go it alone. The areas that we have discussed; Spiritual, Physical, Emotional, Romantic, Mental, Social, and Financial, all have experts. My suggestion is to focus on one area at a time, find the best expert you can afford, and once you have mastered that area move on to the next. If you can't afford to hire an expert for one-on-one coaching, go to a seminar, or on a retreat. If you can't afford an in-person class, find a tele-seminar. If that is out of the budget buy the book, the workbook or any audio files. I recommend mastering these areas of human development in the same order they are outlined in the book. Because all the arenas are connected, you might find that when you clean one area up, a couple others begin to sort themselves out organically.

Be easy on yourself. Beating yourself up will only slow down your growth. Personal development is a process, not an event. Sometimes you will feel stuck. It will feel like you are in a holding pattern and that nothing will ever change. Think of the root of a tree underneath the soil. It appears as though nothing is happening, when you look at the ground and see nothing. But underneath the soil, complex roots are penetrating deep into the earth. If you stay on your path, you might not see results right away. But you are taking on new though-patterns and habits that will produce long term results. In the book "Think and Grow Rich", perhaps the first self-help book ever, Napolean Hill interviewed the wealthiest people in America at that time. He concluded they all had similar characteristics. He also realized that average people share similar values. Only 3% of the population is wealthy. And 97% work for the 3%.

The 3%ers know how to make short term sacrifice for long term gain. Whereas the 97%ers give up if they don't get immediate results. The 3%ers make decisions quickly, based on their gut instinct and change them slowly based on getting their experience. In contrast, the 97%ers make decisions slowly and change their mind quickly. Other people's opinions are why so many average people give up on their dreams. If someone doesn't have the results you want, why would you listen to them? You wouldn't get interior decorating advice from your car mechanic, that's crazy. Well, it's just as silly to get business advice from someone who is not successful in that business. There is a success principal called match and model. Find someone who has what you want, and if you do what they did, you will get what they got. If somebody doesn't have what you want, and they are giving you advice, don't listen to them. Unless you want to have the same lousy result. There are so many self-help books and gurus available. Go seek out the people who have what you want.

Successful people make a decision and stick to it. They are not influenced by other people's opinions. You don't want to be someone who is easily influenced by others. You want to be an influencer. You want to be the person others are reacting to. That is what a leader is. They put their eye on the prize and they do not relent until they achieve it. Like General Patton said, "Lead, follow or get out of the way". Remember that persistence beats resistance. Let's take the worst case scenario and say you don't achieve your goal. At least, you can look back on your life with no regrets. You only regret the chances you don't take. I moved to L.A. to become a famous actor. Although I had the chance to act in network television shows, commercials and feature films, I was not a star. But my soul was sculpted by the process of trying. I met so many people and learned so much about myself and life. If I would have stayed in Ohio, where I am from, and not come to California to go for my acting dream, I would be a totally different person. Now I have different goals and dreams. As you grow and unfold on your path, your dreams may change. But at least have the courage to go for your dreams.

If you have a dream and it's no longer getting you out of bed in the morning and giving you joy, it is time to find a new dream. Life is to be celebrated, not endured. If you are in a job, neighborhood, house, body or relationship that's not getting you excited, then you need to move on. I am not saying to not work on improving certain scenarios. This whole book is about improving each area of your life. But when you have worked so much that it is no longer fun, it's time to cut your losses. I love that Esther and Jerry Hicks used to drive a huge trailer that has a sign, "Life is Supposed to be Fun!" on the side. If you watch children, they are always having fun. Children have boundless energy, adults are constantly relying on caffeine to get them through the day. If you want to have more energy, do things that are fun. Adulting doesn't have to be so droll. What if you found something each day to celebrate?

Whether it's finding a parking spot, having the exact change, or running into an old friend, miracles are happening every day, if we are only aware of them. Most people take these happy coincidences for granted.

Gratitude is the key to happiness. I suggest having a gratitude journal. Try writing just ten things you are grateful for every day and watch your life change. You can enroll all your friends in this gratitude practice by having a group email list. Every day each person writes what they are grateful for and sends it to the group. It is impossible to read what you and all your friends are grateful for and not start to feel better about your life. Gratitude is an attitude. The more grateful you are, the more the Universe will give you to be grateful for. Can you imagine taking a whiny, bratty kid to the store? Every toy they looked at they found something wrong. No toy was good enough. Now imagine taking another kid to the toy store, every toy was their favorite and the best toy ever. They felt so lucky to be in a store with so many amazing toys. Who would you want to buy a toy for? Certainly, not the bratty kid. You wouldn't want to purchase a toy, just for the kid to show you what's wrong with it. You would be motivated to buy toys for the kid who loves everything in the store, because you know how appreciative they would be. They would show you their gratitude for the toys you bought them. You would feel good about yourself. That in turn would motivate you to buy them even more toys.

The Universe works the same way. We are so lucky and blessed in so many ways we don't even acknowledge. We get to work on ourselves and read a book like this. We are not in survival mode, just hoping we don't step on a land mine or get bombed. We are not hungry, wondering when we will have our next meal. We are not struggling with diseases that we could easily cure at our local doctors. We are not worried about getting food poisoning from dirty water or bacteria-laden food. We don't have to go outside to find water to bathe in that might have crocodiles or other predators in it. We have running water. We are able to sleep at night in a quiet room and truly rest. Many people fear so much for their safety that they don't ever enjoy a good night's rest. We have so much to be grateful for that we take for granted every day. The best way to realize how fortunate we are is to be of service to those less fortunate. Find some time to volunteer to help others.

As they say in Al Anon, "give it away for fun and for free." What causes are you passionate about? Do you love children? Volunteer at an orphanage or in a children's cancer ward. Do you care about the environment? Join the Surf Rider Foundation or another group that cleans up the debris polluting our beautiful planet. Do you love animals? You can foster a dog or work in your local animal shelter. Are you concerned with how the elderly are treated? You can go to a nursing home and read to some patients or just spend time with them. Do you worry about the homeless people? You can volunteer at your local soup kitchen. Or you can make paper bag lunches and distribute food to them. There are so many causes that need your help. I have never walked away from being of service to someone and felt down. The opposite is true, whenever I have been of service to the less fortunate, I have realized that all my problems are of my own making. That most people would kill for such luxury problems. These are called First World problems.

You don't have to volunteer to be of service. You can be of service every waking moment by just making a decision to be a force for good in the world. You can make it your daily goal to uplift every single person that crosses your path that day. Whether it be by a smile, a compliment or just being a good listener. So many people just want to be heard. You don't have to provide any advice. Just to listen and connect to a human being is a huge gift. We are in a high technology society where we interact less and less with other people. Technology has helped our society in many ways. But we still have the basic human need of feeling connected to another human or to a community of real people, not just their social media handle. If you are at a party where everyone is staring at their phones, you can be of service just by asking someone how they are feeling today. Most people would rather have a stimulating conversation, than stare at their phone. You can take it upon yourself to start it. People are more attracted to who you are, than what you do or how many followers you have on social media.

That's what this book is about. It's about being your best self in all areas. If you are being your best self, you can be a light in the world. The world is looking for you to SHINE!!! You have dimmed your light long enough. You now have some more tools to burn bright by being your best self. Go for it!

ABOUT THE AUTHOR

Rebecca Whitman is originally from Cincinnati, Ohio and currently resides in Los Angeles, California. She graduated from Princeton University with a degree in English Literature and Italian Language and Culture. As an Executive Director for the direct marketing company Equinox International she developed and trained a sales force of over one thousand individuals in 14 national offices. She was ranked number 3 out of 100,000 sales representative in personal sales volume. She went on to be a top producer at *Mike Davidson Ford* dealership in Jacksonville, Florida, where she helped them to develop new marketing strategies for their internet marketing division.

She moved on to the internet start-up company, *FreeTaxPrep.com*, where she was the Vice President of Business Development. In this company she not only exceeded her quarterly sales quota by 425%, she also hired and trained a sales team that developed a client base of over 281 car dealerships in ten cities in a period of 90 days. As a Talent Coordinator for the *Hollywood Group*, she developed a new marketing strategy that increased the revenue of the company by $250k per year. She achieved between 100% and 400% of her sales quota for the *Hollywood Group*.

As the Vice President of *Sales for Be Entertainment*, she created a sales force that took the company from 0 to $15 million is sales revenue in the first year. She assisted the company's expansion to 7 offices and managed 30 sales reps. She also increased price points from an average of $1400 to $5000 per sale.

Rebecca is currently working for *The Playground-A Young Actor's Conservatory*, where she increased the sales revenue of the company by $1 million per year for 5 consecutive years. In addition to her business acumen, Rebecca has done extensive study in the area of metaphysics with such great teachers as Michael Bernard Beckwith, Esther Hicks, and Marianne Williamson. She has delved into the study of personal relationships with Dr. Pat Allen, Allison Armstrong, and *Landmark Education*. In addition, Rebecca has over 25 years of experience in the 12 Steps. She is also a professionally trained, SAG actress who has appeared in plays, television shows, commercials and movies.

Made in the USA
Middletown, DE
01 June 2021

40811526R00051